Water Habitats

Coral Reefs

JoAnn Early Macken

Reading consultant: Susan Nations, M. Ed.,
author, literacy coach, consultant

WR WEEKLY READER
EARLY LEARNING LIBRARY

Please visit our web site at: www.earlyliteracy.cc
For a free color catalog describing Weekly Reader® Early Learning Library's list
of high-quality books, call 1-877-445-5824 (USA) or 1-800-387-3178 (Canada).
Weekly Reader® Early Learning Library's fax: (414) 336-0164.

Library of Congress Cataloging-in-Publication Data

Macken, JoAnn Early, 1953-
    Coral reefs / JoAnn Early Macken.
      p. cm. — (Water habitats)
    Includes bibliographical references and index.
    ISBN 0-8368-4883-7 (lib. bdg.)
    ISBN 0-8368-4890-X (softcover)
    1. Coral reef ecology—Juvenile literature. I. Title.
QH541.5.C7M344   2005
578.77'89—dc22   2005042278

This edition first published in 2006 by
Weekly Reader® Early Learning Library
A Member of the WRC Media Family of Companies
330 West Olive Street, Suite 100
Milwaukee, WI 53212 USA

Art direction: Tammy West
Cover design and page layout: Kami Koenig
Picture research: Diane Laska-Swanke

Picture credits: Cover, p. 7 © Mark Conlin/SeaPics.com; pp. 5, 9, 21 © Graeme Teague;
pp. 11, 17 © Doug Perrine/SeaPics.com; p. 13 © Mark Strickland/SeaPics.com;
p. 15 © DR & TL Schrichte/SeaPics.com; p. 19 © Jeremy Stafford-Deitsch/SeaPics.com

Printed in the United States of America

1 2 3 4 5 6 7 8 9 09 08 07 06 05

Note to Educators and Parents

Reading is such an exciting adventure for young children! They are beginning to integrate their oral language skills with written language. To encourage children along the path to early literacy, books must be colorful, engaging, and interesting; they should invite the young reader to explore both the print and the pictures.

Water Habitats is a new series designed to help children read about the plants and animals that thrive in and around water. Each book describes a different watery environment and some of its resident wildlife.

Each book is specially designed to support the young reader in the reading process. The familiar topics are appealing to young children and invite them to read — and reread — again and again. The full-color photographs and enhanced text further support the student during the reading process.

In addition to serving as wonderful picture books in schools, libraries, homes, and other places where children learn to love reading, these books are specifically intended to be read within an instructional guided reading group. This small group setting allows beginning readers to work with a fluent adult model as they make meaning from the text. After children develop fluency with the text and content, the book can be read independently. Children and adults alike will find these books supportive, engaging, and fun!

— Susan Nations, M.Ed., author, literacy coach,
and consultant in literacy development

A coral is a group of animals. The animals are called **polyps**. Some corals look like plants. Some look like fingers or brains.

Some polyps grow stony cups to live in. These cups can form a **reef**. A reef can be miles long. It looks like rocks in the water.

Sponges grow on the reef.
Seaweed grows on the reef.
Tiny plants called **algae**
grow there, too.

sponge

Parrotfish eat the algae. They chew the coral, too. They grind it into sand. Their teeth look like birds' beaks.

Eels live in the reef.
They hide in holes in
the coral. They slip
out to hunt for food.

A sea star crawls over the reef. Some sea stars eat coral. Others eat oysters or clams.

sea star

coral

15

A seahorse holds onto the reef. Its mouth is like a straw. It sucks food from the water.

A shark swims near the reef. It hunts for **prey**, small fish to eat.

shark

Small fish dart in and out. Their colors make them hard to see. Their shapes help them fit into cracks. A reef is a good place to hide!

Glossary

algae — tiny plants. Algae help stony corals build their cups and hold the reef together.

clams — animals with soft bodies inside hard, hinged shells. Clams can burrow, or dig down, into sand.

corals — colonies, or large groups, of coral polyps

eels — long, thin fish that look like snakes

oysters — animals with soft bodies inside hard, hinged shells. Oysters attach to the bottom of the sea or to objects in the water.

reef — a line of coral, rocks, or sand in the water. When stony coral polyps die, their cups, or skeletons, remain. New polyps build their cups on top of the old ones. Over time, they grow into coral reefs.

sponges — animals that live in water. They look like plants. A sponge's skeleton holds water. It can be used for washing. Most sponges used for washing now are made by people.

For More Information

Books

Coral Reef Animals. Animals in Their Habitats (series). Francine Galko (Heinemann Library)

Coral Reefs. First Reports: Nature (series). Susan Heinrichs Gray (Compass Point Books)

Coral Reefs. Geography Starts (series). Claire Llewellyn (Heinemann Library)

Hello, Fish: Visiting the Coral Reef. Sylvia A. Earle (National Geographic)

Web Site

Great Barrier Reef
www.nationalgeographic.com/earthpulse/reef/ reef1_flash.html
Facts and photos from National Geographic

Index

About the Author

JoAnn Early Macken is the author of two rhyming picture books, *Sing-Along Song* and *Cats on Judy*, and many other nonfiction books for beginning readers. Her poems have appeared in several children's magazines. A graduate of the M.F.A. in Writing for Children and Young Adults program at Vermont College, she lives in Wisconsin with her husband and their two sons. Visit her Web site at www.joannmacken.com.